About The Author

Theresa Reiner is a retired school teacher and lives in Pennsylvania. She is married and the mother of two grown children. She enjoys time spent with her three grand-children. She loves the outdoors and camping. Theresa has always enjoyed spending time among the trees in the many parks across the United States.

Meet Tess!

She is seven years old and lives with her parents and two sisters. Katie is her younger sister and is 5 years old. Jessie is her older sister and she is 10 years old. Tess is the middle child. She doesn't have any brothers.

Tess Wants To Be A Tree

By Theresa Reiner

Illustrations by Sara Quagliata

Sometimes Tess likes to be alone so she will often go to the backyard and play among the trees.

She likes to bring her tea set to the yard and pretend to have a party with all of her animal friends.

Mr. Squirrel is one friend whom she sees quite often in the yard. He especially likes to show up when Tess brings out her Mommy's "Best in the Whole Wide World" peanut butter cookies.

Tess likes to whistle back to the song birds that nest high up in the trees. She never really sees them, but she hears them and she likes the company.

There are two very large trees that Tess loves to settle between when she has her tea party. They both have flowing leaves that look like green rain coming from the sky. Sometimes, the wind takes the leaves and blows them like a veil on a bride or a waterfall that never touches the ground. These trees, her mommy tells her, are called Weeping Willow trees.

One day when Tess was enjoying the breeze of a warm summer day beneath her favorite trees, she overheard her parents talking to Jessie. Mommy and Daddy were at the kitchen table where most of the family meetings happen. The breeze carried their conversation to Tess through the open window and screen door.

Mommy and Daddy were talking with Jessie about what she wants to be when she grows up. Many exciting ideas were discussed. Jessie thought she might want to be a nurse, a teacher, a singer, a chef, and even an interpreter. An interpreter is someone who learns a new language to help people communicate with each other. Tess thought how exciting it would be to help people understand each other's conversations.

¡Hola!

After a while, Tess decided to go inside to offer her thoughts of what she would like to be when she grows up. She ran as fast as she could through the yard past Mr. Squirrel and under the biggest tree in the yard. She opened the screen door with a screech and it slammed behind her with a loud bang!

The slamming door startled everyone in the kitchen. Katie started to cry and Mommy and Daddy seemed very upset. They have told her a million times not to slam that door!

Jessie had that disgusted look on her face like she often does when her little sister interrupts her.

"So, what are you all doing?", asked Tess.

"Well, if you must know EVERYTHING, I am discussing what I want to be when I grow up", blurted Jessie.

Tess walked right past her sister in a proud way. She stopped in front of her parents and asked in excitement, "Would you like to know what I want to be when I get big?"

"Certainly dear, what is it that you are thinking of becoming when you grow up?" asked Daddy.

"Well, I'm not really sure about this," said Tess. "But I really like trees."

"Well, there are lots of things that you can choose from...", Daddy replied.

But before he could finish explaining the options, Tess blurted out, "That's it! I want to be a tree."

When Jessie burst out laughing, it started a chain reaction.

Soon the whole family was laughing.

HA HA HA!   HA HA HA!

HA HA HA!

HA HA HA!

HA HA HA!   HA HA HA!

HA HA HA!   HA HA HA!

That is, everyone but Tess.

Tess hung her head in embarrassment and slowly walked back to the yard.

All she heard behind her was laughing and Jessie yelling after her, "That is impossible, you can't be a tree!"

Tess became angry with the reaction she received from her family. Soon, Daddy and Mommy came out to the yard to discuss what happened.

"My dear, what is it that makes you want to become a tree?" asked Mommy.

Tess replied, "I just really like trees, they do so many good things."

"What kind of things do trees do that are so good?" asked Daddy.

Mommy and Daddy were interested in Tess's explaination of what trees do. Tess hesitated for a moment. Then, she discussed what she loved about trees.

"Well, first they are a home to so many different animals. I know that because I learned it in school," said Tess.

"People like to sit under them and enjoy the sounds they make when the wind blows and the leaves clap together like tiny hands. Also, trees can clean the air. That is especially nice when you are having a tea party with all of your friends", explained Tess.

Mommy and Daddy just looked at each other and smiled at the thought of their little daughter coming up with so many good reasons to be a tree. If only growing up to be a tree could truly happen. They knew that they needed to tell her gently that she could never grow up to be a tree.

"What kind of tree do you think you would like to be when you grow up?" Daddy asked.
Tess thought for a moment, then said with excitement, "I want to be a Weeping Willow tree!"
With all of her reasons to become a tree, Mommy and Daddy understood why Tess would choose a Weeping Willow tree. However, the time had come for them to explain that Tess would never grow up to be a tree.

Katie was at the screen door looking for Mommy to serve her afternoon snack of those "Best in the Whole Wide World" peanut butter cookies. So, Mommy went into the house to tend to Katie while Daddy explained to Tess the sad truth.

"Tess," Daddy said, "you need to know that someday you will grow up to be a smart, kind, ambitious and beautiful woman. You also need to know that you couldn't ever possibly grow up to become a tree."

Tess looked very sad. She wondered what she could be if she couldn't grow up to be something that she really wanted. "However," Daddy said, "I know of a place that we can go that might give you a great idea of what you can be when you grow up!"

Tess was excited about where Daddy was going to take her. "Where are we going, Daddy?" asked Tess. Daddy opened the car door and Tess jumped excitedly into the back seat of the car and quickly put on her seatbelt.

"Oh, you'll see", was all Daddy would tell her.
This was going to be a surprise!

Daddy drove for what seemed like hours as Tess anticipated the journey to this exciting place. Finally, the car pulled into the parking area of the state park. Soon after they arrived, they met Park Ranger Jill. Tess had so many questions about trees.

"How big do they get? What do trees need? How long do they live? What kinds of animals need them to survive in the forest?"

Park Ranger Jill said something that helped Tess with her ultimate future. "You have so many questions, Tess!" said Park Ranger Jill. "You should become a forest ranger when you grow up. Then you could help to preserve the trees and help animals that live in and depend on the forest."

Tess smiled as she realized what she wants to be when she grows up.

Daddy and Tess drove home to tell Mommy what she had seen and learned from Park Ranger Jill.

After telling of her adventures at the park, Tess exclaimed to her family that she was going to grow up to be a forest ranger.

Mommy and Daddy where were so proud to hear that Tess wants to become a person who understands the needs of nature and the world around her.

Tess would someday be a forest ranger!

Design Email of Illustrator
svqdesigns@gmail.com and Instagram @ svqdesigns